Beauty in Balance

A PRACTICAL GUIDE TO ACHIEVING A
BEAUTIFULLY BALANCED LIFE

Written by YOU

(with a little help from Julie Swenson)

www.julieswensonbeauty.com

Cover photography: Russell Heeter

Cover model: Patrizia Cavaliere

Cover hair and makeup: Julie Swenson

Cover design: Laura Severson

Editing: Megan McCarty and Patrick Blackburn

Interior design: Kim Kalina

This book is dedicated to my son,

Evan

I love you 27 sandwiches to
the moon and back.

Acknowledgements

This book is dedicated to my son Evan Swenson,
and is written in honor of
the (late) Jan Kieffer and (late) Charlie Eidem.

Thank you to the contributors and everyone who was involved with this book:
Laura Severson, Kim Kalina, Russell Heeter, Megan McCarty, Katie Dohman,
Maggie Miley Kelly, Taryn Mason, Stephany Wieland, Mary Pokluda,
Laura Ivanova, Patrizia Cavaliere, and Patrick Blackburn.

Thank you to my friends who helped me get my shit together:
Robin Weier, Liz Paulson, Angela Bristow, Tracy Briese, Trina Dart,
Jules Bruff, Mike Nelson, and Mike Brenny.

Thank you to the gals who have been my sounding board for life and business:
Sharon Oswald, Colleen Belmont, Meghan Casey, Jenny Westbrooks,
Andrea Vogel, Cassie Hanson, Carisa Carlson, and Jen Kos.

Thank you to my beauty team who are so amazing in every way:
Dawn Goebel, Amber Brenke, Priscilla Bruce, Lianna Colestock, Katie Pierce,
Jen DesLauriers, Andria Johnson, and Alexis Hamlin-Vogler.

Thank you to my business/life coaches and trainers:
Carrie Lee Kelly, Cindy Lee, and Caroline Adams Miller.

Thank you to the people whom I've met on my travels, who have inspired me
and helped me grow: Sonny, Ike, Julia, and Kirk.

Thank you to my family, friends, colleagues, and frendors for your
unwavering support.

"Beauty begins the moment you decide to be yourself."

- Coco Chanel

Introduction + {Instructions}

I have worked in the beauty industry for 22 years, and throughout that time, one theme has always remained constant—true beauty comes from within. I can't emphasize enough how important it is to treat beauty from the inside out, paying equal attention to the mind, body and spirit. This workbook serves as a practical guide to achieving balance, peace and fulfillment in life. When we are balanced, we are able to be our true selves and live our best lives.

I feel fortunate that I am surrounded by amazing, strong, intelligent women every day. Their stories, thoughts and insight empower me and help me grow as a person. Conversations with my clients and friends stretch beyond beauty. We discuss everything from motherhood to nutrition to yoga poses. These conversations have inspired this guide/workbook/journal.

When I told my friend Liz that I was writing *Beauty in Balance* she responded, "You should practice what you preach."

Ugh. I knew she was right. If I was going to create a workbook about whole body wellness, I'd better make sure I was able to walk the walk. No one wants to discover that the person who is encouraging personal growth is a hot mess.

And boy was I a hot mess.

A few years ago, a divorce and a misguided business deal left me financially and emotionally devastated. I wasn't quite the train wrecks you see on TMZ, but I was close. I realized that, while I had lost almost everything, I still had my self-worth. My integrity, skills and personality were still intact. I learned what I truly valued in life–my family, my friends, my time, my passions and myself. I relied less on "things," recognition and outside validation, and focused more on what type of person I wanted to be. I focused on being a mother, a friend, a mentor and a support to others in my community.

This workbook is living testament of the personal work I went through to get back on my feet, which, admittedly, is still in progress. I owe a debt of gratitude to all of the women in my life who directly or indirectly inspired me to do so.

For some subjects in this workbook, I have relied on other experts to share their experiences. Bringing others into this project affirms the importance of connecting and sharing knowledge. I invite you to get to know the contributors by visiting their websites that are listed on the suggested resources pages.

{Instructions} to using this workbook

Start with the first chapter of this workbook. It's a deep dive into looking at ourselves and taking inventory on how we feel about ourselves and the lives we are creating. It is the foundation of your journey. In the last section, we will measure your progress with a self-evaluation.

I hope you tap into something inspiring with this workbook. I invite you to use it in any way that serves you best. There is no judgment, no deadline and no expectations. The only thing I ask is that, throughout your journey, you remain honest and kind to yourself.

Love,
Julie

Thoughts

"Know thyself."

- Socrates

You + {Self}

Hello, beautiful. In this chapter I am going to address six aspects of self that are the cornerstones of this workbook. Start with this chapter before moving on to the next. And if needed, come back to this chapter again (and again!).

The Six Aspects of {Self}:

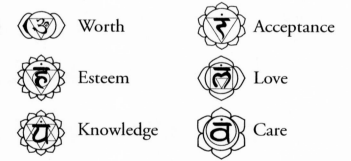

Worth

Acceptance

Esteem

Love

Knowledge

Care

{Self} worth + {Self} esteem

Some would say that self-worth and self-esteem are the same thing. I disagree. Self-worth is an innate belief that we are worthy of love and happiness. Unfortunately, our environment and life circumstances can erode self-worth and can affect how much we value and respect ourselves. We should not fall victim to this, though, as we have the control and the ability to protect and repair our self-worth.

Self-esteem, on the other hand, is the positive and negative thoughts we have about ourselves. This can come from personal evaluation or outside influences, such as other people, and the amount of self-esteem that we have can fluctuate throughout our lives. It's important to protect and be mindful of our self-worth every day while actively maintaining and cultivating our self-esteem (also known as self-confidence and self-assuredness).

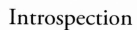

Introspection

On a scale from 1-10, how much do you respect and value yourself? (1 being not at all and 10 being as much as humanly possible)

Write down three things you really dig about yourself:

Write down three things other people really dig about you:

What outside influences affect your self-esteem? How can you remove the negative influences and add more of the positive ones?

{Self} knowledge + {Self} acceptance

These two are my favorite of the "selfs." I am on a constant quest to get to know myself. Call me a narcissist (it's okay, many people have), but I like learning about who I am. It motivates me to grow and become my best possible self.

The more we know about ourselves—our traits, thoughts and behaviors—the more self-aware we become. With this awareness we are able to change and/or manage our thoughts and emotions. Self-awareness is one of the facets of emotional intelligence and an important factor of living a balanced life. When we can navigate our attention, emotions, reactions, personality, and behavior, we put ourselves in the driver's seat of our own lives.

When we have a good grasp of who we are, we become more accepting of ourselves and the world around us. With each stage of our life, we acquire more self-knowledge, which generates more self-acceptance. We reflect, practice introspection, and create a new construct (self-identity). In other words, we simply accept that the past is the past and forge ahead with a stronger sense of self.

Introspection

On a scale from 1-10, how well do you know yourself?
(1 being not that well and 10 being you know yourself pretty
darn well)

Describe who you are in one sentence:

Do you accept yourself as you are right now? Why or why
not?

Do you accept your life as it is right now? Why or why not?

What else can you do to gain more acceptance in your life?
Share both thoughts and actions:

{Self} love + {Self} care

Here's the deal: We cannot love others until we love ourselves first. I know, sometimes it can be difficult for us to love ourselves. Maybe no one taught us how to love, or maybe we're holding on to whatever mistakes we've made in the past. I have good news for you. It's time for all of us to forgive ourselves and move on with our lives.

Simply being mindful of the present is the most helpful practice to let go of the past. Modern Buddhists define mindfulness as an attentive awareness of the present moment. I like to define mindfulness as living in the moment and awakening to our true potential—fully knowing and accepting who we are and living on purpose. Practicing mindfulness has a multitude of health benefits such as reducing stress, increasing focus and strengthening our immune system. Mindfulness is the #1 self-care practice you can do on a daily basis.

But what is self-care exactly? Psychologist, Christine Meinecke, Ph.D., states that, "self-care means choosing behaviors that balance the effects of emotional and physical stressors: exercising, eating healthy foods, getting enough sleep, practicing yoga or meditation or relaxation techniques, abstaining from substance abuse and pursuing creative

{Self} love + {Self} care

outlets."[1] She also states that self-care is not about self-pampering or self-indulgence, like getting pedicures or shopping. It's not about indulging in things that give us instant gratification, but rather doing things that enhance our well-being.

---

1. Meinecke, Christine, Ph.D. "Self care in a toxic world." *psychologytoday.com*. June 4, 2010.

Introspection

On a scale from 1-10, how much do you love yourself?
(1 being not so much and 10 being maybe you're a narcissist)

What can you do to increase your number?

What percentage of your day-to-day thoughts are about the past? 10%, 30%, 50%, 70%, 100%?

What do you need to let go of in order to move forward?

How are you currently practicing self-care?

Write down one new self-care practice that you will begin doing today:

Our physical, mental, spiritual and emotional well-being all depend on self-care. When we neglect one element, we become out of balance. The next 11 chapters will help you create a beautifully balanced life. At the end of this workbook, there is a self-evaluation page. The ultimate goal is personal growth, so if you finish this whole book and don't feel any different or better about yourself and your life, well, I guess I'll give you your money back. (Just kidding, all sales are final.)

Suggested Resources

Books:

The Gifts of Imperfection: Let Go of Who You Think You're Supposed to Be and Embrace Who You Are by Brene Brown

Love Yourself Like Your Life Depends On It by Kamal Ravikant

Websites:
- allwomenstalk.com
- self.com

Apps:
- Stress Free with Deepak Chopra
- Transform Your Life

Gratitude + {Perspective}

I thought I was a grateful person. But turns out I was faking gratitude, pretending to appreciate everything in my life when secretly I was wanting more, more and some more.

I had a slight chip on my shoulder and a huge ego.

I am not necessarily referring to the ego as an overinflated sense of self; rather the ego that is a separation of our self from our soul. The ego that dictates our thoughts and emotions and cares about possessions and status and how others perceive us. The ego that identifies with our made-up self instead our true self. The ego that thrives off of fear and insecurities. Yeah, that ego.

When I first started doing weddings, I operated out of a fear-based ego. I wasn't sure of my abilities and my thoughts were self-serving. What was I going to get out of the wedding? What type of validation and recognition was I going to receive?

Then I met Amber. She was the first person I hired to help me at weddings. Ten years younger than me with an insane amount of raw talent, she quickly made a name for herself. I could have been resentful. I could have been jealous. But instead, Amber taught me two valuable lessons in life and in business:

1. Shed the ego, or be controlled by it.
2. Practice humility daily.

I knew that if I worked on overcoming my ego, then I would be free of thoughts that could cause negative behaviors and hinder my growth as well as other people's success.

I started focusing on my own skills instead of comparing myself to others. I began honing in on my purpose and my calling. I developed something new to me, something called humility—a humble awareness of one's place in the world.

I learned to keep my ego in check and practice humility. Now it's no longer about how the brides can validate my work and me; it's more about what I can do for them.

On my busy weekends when I have three or more weddings, which means high expectations for me to perform at my best, I start my day with meditation. I think about how grateful I am for the work, for the opportunity to be a part of such an amazing life event, and set an intention. It's important to me to bring the best energy into a room for the bride on her wedding day.

Being grateful is essential to living a fulfilling and balanced life. When we're grateful, we tend to focus on the things that we have rather than the things that we don't. It takes introspection, perspective and humility to achieve a true state of gratitude.

Introspection is the ability to consciously examine our thoughts and feelings. It only takes a few minutes to slow the mind down, hone in on our emotions and learn more about the inner workings of our mind, body and soul. The self-knowledge we gain from introspection can influence our worldview, also known as our perspective. By looking inward and expanding and evolving our beliefs and attitudes, we can easily shift our perspective and paradigms.

When we gain perspective, we gain humility. This opens us up to be in a conscious and constant state of gratitude.

Drawing upon the law of attraction—the belief that "like attracts like"—when we make it a habit of being grateful, we attract more things to be grateful for.

gratitude + {perspective}

Our daily practice of gratitude can be as easy as waking up thinking, I am grateful for all that I have. We can expand on that by creating a gratitude journal, giving more sincere compliments, lessening complaints, volunteering our time to a person or cause we care about and practicing present-moment gratitude.

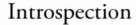

Introspection

On a scale from 1-10, how grateful are you right now?
(1 being zero/zilch and 10 being your cup runneth over)

9

Take a moment to be introspective about a current situation
and/or person in your life (a relationship, job, child). What
are the first thoughts and emotions that come to mind? Let
your inner monologue run wild and write your stream of
consciousness here:

Bella, sweet loving
Miguel, stubarn, loving, caring
My kids, I love them so much
and I'm very happy / grateful
for both, yet I find myself
looking for Breaks from them
every now and then.

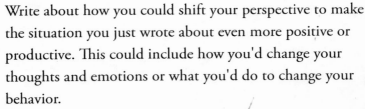

Write about how you could shift your perspective to make the situation you just wrote about even more positive or productive. This could include how you'd change your thoughts and emotions or what you'd do to change your behavior.

By looking for ways/things to do with them and enjoying the time we spend together.

Write down five things/people you are grateful for right now and why:

Miguel –
Bella –
My job –
my health –
My Friends –

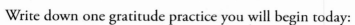

Write down one gratitude practice you will begin today:

End of the day / Before bed
write down things I'm
grateful for.

Write down one gratitude practice you will begin tomorrow:

Give more compliments.

Write a thank you card or letter to someone who has been a positive influence in your life. It doesn't have to be long, but be specific with the reasons why you appreciate this person. Who will you write to? When will you mail it?

Today.
Julie

Suggested Resources

Books:

A Simple Act of Gratitude by John Kralik

Humilitas: A Lost Key to Life, Love, and Leadership by John Dickson

Websites:
- tinybuddha.com
- gratitudehabit.com

Apps:
- Gratitude Journal 365 Pro
- Gratitude Stream

"Love yourself enough to live a healthy lifestyle."

- Unknown

Health + {Wellness}

Some things we have total control over, like preventative health measures to avoid issues in the future. But sometimes you go to the gynecologist and find out that you have a brain tumor.

When I was 26, I went off the birth control pill. I didn't menstruate for eight months. A little worried, I told my friend Liz and she responded, "Dude, that's not normal. Go see a doctor."

I went to the clinic and they did some blood work. The results came back that my prolactin level was too high. (What the eff is prolactin? Google it.) Then the doctor told me it might mean that I have a pituitary brain tumor.

Wait. What?

I freaked out and immediately started researching it online, finding horror stories of others with the same condition going blind or losing their pituitary functions.

How did this happen? I'd never had a health issue in my life other than the common cold. I went in for an MRI, which they had to sedate me for because I don't get excited about small X-ray machines.

They identified that there was indeed a tumor. Thankfully, it was benign. I was put on medication to see if the tumor would shrink. It did not.

I asked my University of Minnesota doctor if I could get a second opinion. She referred me to the Mayo Clinic in Rochester, Minnesota.

I met with their endocrinologist and neurosurgeon who both suggested surgery. Then, in 2008, I had the tumor removed. It was a quick recovery and now I just have to do an MRI every few years to ensure the tumor hasn't returned.

Not everyone gets a wake-up call like that early in life. It changed the way I viewed my life. It made me realize that I am not as invincible as I thought. There really is a beginning and an end to life.

Up to that point in my life, I had taken my health for granted. But from then on I was motivated to make the necessary changes to ensure a longer, healthier life.

I began researching ways to stay healthy and get stronger. Honestly, I am not an extremely active person and I don't always eat the healthiest. (Damn you, pasta and chocolate!) What worked for me was finding the right combination of foods and exercise, taking on a whole-body approach of nourishing my mind, body and spirit.

I started to pay close attention to what nourishment I was putting into my body, and began eating superfoods--nutrient-rich foods that are packed with large doses of antioxidants, polyphenols, vitamins, and minerals. I began practicing yoga and meditation again, and learned a specific breathing technique called *pranayama*. Having experienced this type of lifestyle shift leads me to believe that **the key to finding the motivation** to eat well and exercise is to **customize what works for you**.

I could cite all of the best-selling books on food and exercise, but the list would be overwhelming. First, start by connecting with a personal fitness trainer or a health coach that aligns with your health philosophy and wellness goals. This is a great way to determine what food and exercise is best for you.

I had the opportunity to speak with Taryn Mason, a certified health coach who takes a spiritual approach to weight loss and nutrition. I was inspired by her story. Struggling with her own weight loss and self-esteem, Taryn did some soul-searching and discovered that her greatest obstacle was herself. (Which, for most people, is the case.) When she learned to truly love and nourish herself, that's when her life changed. Her mantra is *I'm enough, you're enough.*

Q + A
with Taryn Mason

**What is the difference between a health coach, a
nutritionist and a registered dietitian (RD)?**

Health coaches play a different role in health and wellness
than a registered dietician or a nutritionist. We understand
that health and weight loss extends beyond food and into all
areas of life including relationships, career, physical activity,
and spirituality. A health coach will guide you through
identifying your vision and will provide tools and accountability for making sustainable actions towards your life's goals.
We also have an understanding of a broad spectrum of dietary
theories and help you find a way of eating that works for your
unique mind, body, soul and lifestyle. Above all else, we
understand that you have the ability to heal yourself, by
yourself, when blocks and resistance are removed and offer the
unconditional love and support necessary for lasting change.

Registered dieticians (RDs) take a more scientific approach to
nutrition. They typically work in clinical settings and write
meal plans for people who suffer from a specific ailment. They
focus on the role of macro and micronutrients in the body in
relation to disease. They aren't looking holistically at aligning

the rest of your life. A health coach could work alongside RDs to ensure implementation of the plan.

Nutritionist is a broad term that could apply to someone working in a clinical setting, food manufacturing or someone who is administering a diet plan to individuals. Again, they aren't necessarily looking at the bigger picture of your life and what is getting in the way of implementing what you already know deep down inside.

Can you tell us about your own health journey?
I can't remember a time when I wasn't on a diet or thinking I needed to be on a diet. I grew up in a "we'll start dieting again Monday" household and wasted so much time and energy in a gym, in a state of deprivation or gluttony, and feeling like a failure over and over again.

Because I didn't feel perfect.
I messed it all up.
My willpower wasn't strong enough.

"I blew it on that meal, I might as well throw in the towel."

I was extremely hard on myself. All. The. Time. I was afraid to try anything new if I didn't know I could be the best at it.

If a diet didn't work, something was wrong with *me*, not the diet. My body was failing me.

If I failed, *I* was a failure.

Years of poor nutrition, (attempted) calorie restriction, excessive exercise, chronic stress and a constant beating from my thoughts caught up to me in the form of hypothyroidism, IBS, and yo-yo weight fluctuations.

Doctors told me food had nothing to do it. They were wrong. But they were also right.

I began to explore using real, whole foods as a way to heal my body and I finally felt as though I "got it." I finally knew how to lose weight!

I was practicing yoga, coaching wellness cleanse programs, and eating perfectly clean, whole foods free of toxins, and allergens. I had an abundance of energy, released excess weight and improved my thyroid levels. Everything seemed to come together. I tasted what it was like to be the number on the scale I so desperately needed to be before I could be happy with myself.

But I still didn't feel good enough. So why didn't I feel fulfilled? Why did I still feel like food controlled me? Why was I dreaming of pizza, cookies, and French fries? What was the missing link? *Is kale not the key to happiness?* Was it that even in a thinner body, my mind still obsessed over my weight? Could it be true that the story I had been telling myself–"when I'm thin or perfect enough, I'll be able to _____"–isn't actually true? I was still hard on myself and nothing was ever enough. Was there something else missing for me to be enough?

I found my answer a few years later while traveling around the world with NO health goals. *Gasp!* It awakened within me the idea of what was missing–a connection with my soul. I blocked it for so many years because I'm so sensitive and intuitive, because I feel *everything*. I was controlling the symptoms–weight and body image–rather than addressing the real issue: disconnection from soul and all that is inherently enough.

I was living this amazing life full of adventure and wonderful relationships. Why didn't I love myself? Why did I care so much about my weight or size or belly fat or what other people thought? I was the same person on the inside no matter what was on the scale and I needed to love her unconditionally and nourish her and share her. Then. Now.

What a life-altering decision! Who knew that taking care of myself would unlock so many amazing opportunities and create space for growth, expansion, new adventures, fulfilling relationships, and even a new soul-fulfilling career. The years of chronic self-induced stress from ignoring my intuition did a number on my insides both physically and spiritually. The soul (or spirit) is the energy that keeps us alive and contains the higher purpose for life. It feels *really bad* to be disconnected, but the good news is the bad feelings are the guide back home to feeling *really good*–back to glowing from the inside out.

It feels amazing to be reunited with soul and a higher purpose. We're not a number on a scale or a clothing tag. We're not our diet and exercise routine. We have so much to offer this world and I am on a mission to help women find their freedom from the perfection trap and chronic dieting. *Soulful* weight loss is moving from restriction to abundance, perfection to enough, self-loathe to self-love. It's not at all about finding religion or following more rules. It's about choosing love over fear in all areas of life, following your own intuition and watching the weight fall away in the wake of inspiration, and an abundance of energy to create a full, vibrant life on your terms that *feels really good*.

What are your philosophies on food and eating?
I grew up on a diet of processed foods, meat and potatoes, and cereal and toast for breakfast; constantly counting the calories I was consuming. Ordering pizza on a Friday night meant we were able to let loose a little, before starting a diet again on Monday. I worried constantly about weight, and it felt like prison. I didn't start feeling and seeing physical results until I ditched the calorie counting in lieu of eating real, whole, unprocessed foods. Even then I tried a variety of "diets" claiming to be healthier, but science is catching up with my own conclusion that no diet will work in the long run, even if it's touted as "healthy". I continued to slip back into old habits and the yo-yo cycle. I didn't see permanent results until I improved my relationship with food, began to trust myself around food, and focused on fueling my soul rather than following a perfect diet.

Following a set of complicated rules, relying on restriction and willpower, and cutting out entire food groups will never work for long-term health and vitality because it takes *you* out of the equation. No amount of kale will make a difference if you're not connected to *you*. Your mind and body won't learn how to eat when you're hungry and stop when you're done if you're following someone else's way of eating. This sets you up for failure.

We are inundated each day with so many different diets and conflicting information about nutrition but no one knows better than you what your body needs to heal and thrive. *Soul-fueling* does not have to be as complicated as it's made out to be. To start, my philosophy would include a variety of real, whole foods (no label or one-ingredient labels), an abundance of plants, and nuts and seeds.

I believe in empowered eating—eating from choice and noticing how it makes you feel. Your body will give you clues about what it needs in the form of feelings, cravings, and (in)digestion. Each meal is a chance to check in with what it is you're truly hungry for and give your body what it needs.

Is what's on your plate going to feel good, or will it simply taste good? Does it excite the soul and bring passion back to your life? Is it bringing joy either through the sensual experience or the company with whom it's shared? What are your cravings telling you about what your body needs more or less of? Are your eyes bright and skin glowing? Do you feel like you can move mountains or do you need a nap?

Empowered eating is making a conscious choice at every meal. It means eating the berries because you want to, because it feels good and tastes good to do so. It does not mean following a perfect plan or depriving yourself of anything. You check in before eating the cake. If you truly want it, you eat it from an empowered place, rather than mindlessly shoving the whole thing down because after one piece you might as well keep going. (Been there!)

It means checking in with your hunger, eating when you're hungry, eating what you're hungry for, and stopping when you've had enough. No rules, no perfection, just listening to what feels good and adding more of that. Because what *feels good* is your clue from the soul.

What are your philosophies on exercise?
There is no magic formula for exercise, just like there's no magic formula for eating. You can't exercise your way out of a poor diet. Using exercise as a way to justify the junk or punish yourself is the quickest way to sabotage even the best efforts.

I've tried as many workout programs as I have diets. Most led to injury and burnout because I wasn't listening to my body and pushed beyond my limits in order to burn more calories. It is so easy to fall into a trap of thinking weight loss and health is based on calories. This is the most soul-sucking mindset you can get wrapped into, and unfortunately obesity rates continue to rise because of it. If you get really honest with yourself, when has eating less and exercising more *ever* worked for permanent weight loss and feeling of wellness and vitality?

There *is* a kinder, more effective approach to exercise. Our bodies actually want to move when we remove the obstacles and resistance. Moving in a way that *feels good* (are you picking up on a theme here?) will be much more impactful than the latest infomercial exercise craze or killing yourself in the gym. Not just because of consistency, but because if it feels good, your body will remain in a relaxed state.

It is in this relaxed state that healing and releasing can begin. Forcing exercise or over-exercising adds excess stress to the body. This is bad for health and more importantly it is bad for your soul.

Soulful movement makes it fun to try new things, find challenge in a way that breaks through fears and limiting beliefs, and builds self-trust and confidence. Exercise is a powerful tool to improve community and provide social interaction – all good for the soul. *Let the spirit move you.*

My philosophy is to bring fun and love into everything you do. Our bodies can do more than our minds think, but forcing the body into something leads to stress, injury, rebellion and often inaction. Aligned movement catapults you to a whole new level when it combines a multi-sensory experience that calms your presence and creates a relaxed state of mind and body.

Find your relaxed state and soar. This is the key to soulful, *feel-good* living. When you're in the present moment, you are more aligned with your soul, which is truly unlimited. Fuel the soul in everything you do and you can't be wrong. Learn to listen to your body and follow your intuition; it will not mislead you.

Why is it difficult for people to stay consistent with mindful eating and exercise?

We are taught to push, force, and make things happen—to muscle our way through life with something to prove. It can be scary to switch the mindset back to trusting the body and soul and resist the urge to force something into existence, but to allow ease and relaxation to heal.

Attempting to make well-intentioned, sweeping changes without an aligned plan or support, and trying to follow someone else's rules, are the biggest reasons why it could be hard to remain consistent. Making changes that bypass your internal guidance system will not last. I have been there over and over again.

Rules that create an impression of being on- or off-track set you up for an all-or-nothing approach. You are always "on track." This is your life. *Your* life. What choices are you making and how do they make you feel? Are they aligned with your vision? Do you have support?

Empowered eating (and living) resonates with me so much more than mindful eating. I attempted mindful eating several times. I was mindful of the fact that I was sitting on the couch downing an entire large pizza, but it didn't stop me. I just thought, *"Hmmm, I know this isn't really what I want to be eating right now, but I can't stop."*

Eating out of alignment with your body and soul, not being fully empowered in choice, and following someone else's rules—even if done mindfully—won't feel good and therefore won't stick.

Part of my role as your health coach is to show you how to begin following your intuition by interpreting the body's signals, what alignment feels like, and how to be curious about cravings. I help you make the small, sustainable changes and mindset shifts that allow healthy, aligned habits to stick for a lifetime.

You focus on the mind, body and spirit. Why is a holistic approach important?

The holistic approach is important because everything in life is connected and cannot be "fixed" in silos. Getting a good night's sleep makes it easier to eat from an empowered place of fueling the body with nutrients and love. Eating well makes it easier to exercise, and moving throughout the day makes it easier to sleep and eat well, further improving the cycle.

We are fueled by so much more than sleep, food, and physical activity. Your relationships, community, spirituality and creativity also impact your overall energy, stress levels, and ability to eat from an empowered place.

What you choose to engage in each day either increases your energy or drains it. You might be more prone to reach for the sugary snacks in the afternoon because your energy is depleted by a soul-sucking career or environment. Being immobilized on the couch in resistance to the gym will influence your dinner choice.

Your thoughts create your reality so if you're worrying about one thing in your life, it will spill over into your choices in every other area.

The only thing that helped me find my way towards sustainable weight loss and boundless energy was to look at fueling my soul in all areas of life. What felt good deep down was being in alignment with who I really am at my core—peace, love, and joy. Being in alignment and feeling good in all areas of life helps with empowered food choices, movement, and sleep. So many people think that controlling their diet and exercise will make them feel better, and they won't look internally for the answers. We aren't taught any differently.

Is there a relationship between self-love and wellness?
Self-love *is* wellness. You can't have one without the other and both are your birthright. Recognizing this deep in my soul is what finally broke my own "not-enough" pattern. It released me from the diet trap and into a real solution that felt good in my soul. I made the conscious choice to love myself unconditionally every day and I will never turn back. Everything has changed from this one action.

What does self-love mean exactly? It looks like radical self-care and is the most selfless thing you can choose to do. It means in every moment bringing the mind back to loving, positive thoughts, kindness, and treating your mind, body, and soul with respect. Eating from a place of love, loving what you eat. Moving from a place of love, loving how you move. Living from a place of love, loving how you live. Life begins to flow with ease from this place of love. You start to see more of what you want and feeling how you want to feel. It feels like magic. You begin to glow from the inside out.

I once heard a speaker say that you don't need a reason to love yourself—you just have to remember to do it. This really resonated with me. I spent so much of my life proving to myself and others that I was worthy of love, when the truth was I was inherently worthy. I am love. *You* are love.

You help women overcome the "not-enoughness" feeling. Tell us more and how you do this.
Ultimately I hold a big bubble of love and possibility for women to reconnect with their own soul, in whatever way resonates for them. Our souls hold the truth of who we are and contains limitless, infinite energy. It is pure love and at the core of each of you. It gives you spark and passion. It is the energy of well-being and available at all times.

Diet and exercise are simply more ways to remind you that it's not enough to be who you are, and this is a lie. The pursuit of anything outside of you for validation is another way to jockey for worthiness. You are at your core enough, and when you believe this can be true a whole new reality opens up with unlimited possibilities. I know this with all of my heart and soul to be true. There is nothing to prove, you are inherently enough, and part of why you're here on the planet is to discover who you really are.

Any negative thought that you have about yourself, or any bad feeling can be a clue to what's out of alignment with who you really are. And who you really are is joy and love. This is why doing what feels good is so important. It's a no shame, no blame game, but it can be tricky to navigate without support. I help sort through the tricks of the brain that keep you safe so you can find your truth and freedom. It feels so good to reconnect you with *you*. It feels right. It feels like peace.

What's your favorite quote?
"Peace. It does not mean to be in a place where there is no noise, trouble or hard work. It means to be in the midst of those things and still be calm in your heart." - Unknown

Tell us something about health and wellness we may not know.

Beauty, health, and wellness truly come from within, from being connected with your soul, spirit, essence, God—whatever language resonates. Well-being is your birth-right and is always present in your soul, holding the key to your best and highest self. Being present in soul energy is so light and bright it beams out of every pore in the body, sparkles in the eyes, glows through the skin, radiates love out into the world. It *feels* good.

Introspection

On a scale from 1-10, how physically fit are you? (1 being you live in leggings and 10 being I could punch you in the gut and it wouldn't hurt)

What are you currently doing for your physical fitness? Do you like what you're doing? Why or why not?

What type of physical activity haven't you explored yet, or maybe need to re-discover? (Examples: cross country skiing, yoga, barre, zumba, pilates, sex)

What are three life circumstances (obstacles) that prevent you from physical activities or are preventing you from doing it more often?

What are two ways to overcome the obstacles to give you more time or inspiration to be physical?

Do you have an accountability partner? Who is it and what does he/she do for you? (If not, well…maybe you should find one.)

What is one new exercise that you can put into motion today? (Think squats, kegels, etc.)

On a scale from 1-10, how healthy do you eat? (1 being you consider diet soda a food group and 10 being you love to graze on grass)

If you're lower on the scale, are you interested in increasing your number? If yes, why? If no, why not? If you're higher on the scale are you interested in staying where you are or increasing the number? If yes, why, and if no, why not?

What healthy foods are you currently enjoying?

What healthy foods have you been wanting to try?

What are your "I don't care what you have to say Julie, I'll never give these up" foods?

What are the three life circumstances (obstacles) that prevent you from eating healthier?

What are two ways to overcome the obstacles to help you eat healthier?

How do you hold yourself accountable when it comes to the food you eat?

Suggested Resources

Books:

The China Study: The Most Comprehensive Study of Nutrition Ever Conducted And the Startling Implications for Diet, Weight Loss, And Long-term Health by Thomas Campbell

Eat to Live Cookbook: 200 Delicious Nutrient-Rich Recipes for Fast and Sustained Weight Loss, Reversing Disease, and Lifelong Health by Joel Fuhrman

Websites:
- mindbodygreen.com
- prevention.com

Apps:
- Shopwell–Healthy Diet and Grocery Food Scanner
- Restaurant Nutrition

Taryn Mason's info:
- Website: tarynmason.com
- Facebook: facebook.com/tarynjmason
- Twitter: @nutritaryn
- Instagram: @soulfulweightloss
- Pinterest: pinterest.com/tarynjmason

Thoughts

"...do something that improves your life and the lives of those you love."

- Maria Nemeth

Money + {Finance}

When my life hit the skids from a divorce and a misguided business deal, I was thrown off of my center big time. I was out of control. I wasn't a total train wreck, or a complete disaster; I was more like a ship wreck, with parts of me floating about aimlessly.

My financial fitness took a hit during that time because of circumstances out of my control, yes, but also because I did not have a healthy relationship with money.

Our relationship with money is one of the most important relationships we'll have in our life.

That is why it's imperative to treat money like we would a spouse, best friend or family member: with love, respect, commitment, gratitude and accountability.

Building a healthy relationship with money begins with understanding it. Money is an energetic entity. We give it life with our actions and intentions. Every time we give and receive money, we are connecting or disconnecting with its energetic life force.

We need to be mindful of how we manage that energy and our money. We also need to ask ourselves what purpose it serves in our lives. When we get to know our dear friend money, that's when we become fully conscious of our fiscal thoughts, emotions and behaviors.

Right now it's not about wishing we had more, or trying to live on less. Today it's about making peace with our current finances and being grateful for what we have. Accepting what we have or the lack of what we have in savings, checking and inheritance. Embracing our salary, our home value, our 401(k) balance and acknowledging our debts.

Our new relationship with money starts now.

Introspection

On a scale from 1-10, how mindful are you with your money?
(1 being impulsive and 10 being practical)

Write down one practice that you can do to improve your
current financial situation and when you will do it:

What purpose does money have in your life? (What does
money do for you physically, spiritually, emotionally and
intellectually?)

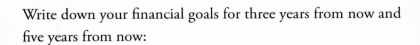

Write down your financial goals for three years from now and five years from now:

How can you further educate yourself on financial fitness?

Beyond the necessities, what are you spending your money on that keeps you in balance and increases your self-worth?

What advice would you give a child about money management?

Suggested Resources

Books:

The Total Money Makeover: A Proven Plan for Financial Fitness by Dave Ramsey

The Energy of Money: A Spiritual Guide to Financial and Personal Fulfillment by Maria Nemeth, Ph.D.

Websites:
- dailyworth.com
- girlsjustwannahavefunds.com

Apps:
- Money and the Law of Attraction Cards
- Mint Personal Finance

Thoughts

"Being a mother is not about what you gave up to have a child, but what you've gained from having one." - Unknown

Motherhood + {Parenting}

From a very young age I thought that I didn't want to have children. Children meant sacrifice and hard work. I was way too selfish and self-involved to give up my life for someone else.

Friends and boyfriends would always be surprised of my desire *not* to have children, expressing, "What? You'd be a great mom!"

But what makes a great mom? What were they seeing in me that would make them believe I could handle the responsibility of shaping a human being and giving up my free-spirited lifestyle? Well, imagine everyone's surprise when I did, in fact, have a child. In the first year of my marriage, my husband lost his father to a motorcycle crash. It was devastating. He wanted to fill the void his father left by starting a family of his own.

At first I was a very anxious, nervous mother. I would obsess over every thing I did or didn't do. I remember insisting on getting the carpets cleaned because I was convinced they were poisonous and would harm baby Evan. (Because babies tend to lick carpets, right?) I was driving my husband-and myself!-crazy trying to be perfect.

After a year of being a basket case, my husband sat me down and gave me the best parenting advice I ever received: "You don't have to be a perfect mom, you just have to be a good enough mom. All we need to give Evan is **warmth, acceptance, love, and guidance**, and he'll turn out fine."

I took the advice to heart, and in those moments when I am about to lose my mind, I repeat the mantra in my head: **warmth, acceptance, love, and guidance**. I'm still not a perfect mom, but I am a much calmer mom than I used to be. And I believe that when I am centered, my child is centered. Children really do mirror our thoughts, emotions, and behaviors. They are modeling exactly what they see.

I'll never regret having a child. I love being a mom. I was right, parenting is hard work, but I was wrong about the sacrifice. Being a mother is not about what you gave up to have a child, but what you've gained from having one. I've gained a person who inspires me and challenges me, who helps me recognize my strengths and honestly helps me be a better person. I just hope I can do as much in this lifetime for Evan as he has done for me.

In addition to loving motherhood, I love the sisterhood that I have with other mothers. I can't tell you how many times I've called my friends in a frenzy. "My son just ate a chicken nugget that's been sitting out for 10 hours!" (Okay, that only happened once and my son survived.)

Being part of parent communities, live and online, has given me immense support and camaraderie. When I can relate to the same fears, joys, and having "one of those days," it makes me feel like we're all in this together. There's truth in the African proverb: "It takes a village to raise a child." It's important for us to reach out to others for support and friendship. Reading parenting blogs, magazines, and books are a wonderful resource and provide some comic relief in our often routine and serious lives.

One writer in particular, Katie Dohman, provides great insight about parenting in a light, humorous and thoughtful way. She views parenting as an adventure and fully embraces all that it entails-like sleep deprivation and how stressful it can be to take a simple day trip with a toddler. While she may not label herself as one, Katie is an exceptional role model on how to be a real mom and live a real life with real challenges and real joys.

Q + A
with Katie Dohman

How would you describe your life as a mom in one sentence?

Crazy chaotic amazingness.

What's the one thing about motherhood that you know now that you wish someone would have told you about before your daughter was born?

You know, I think people tell you this, but you just have no way of really, really knowing until it happens to you. Your capacity and the fierceness of the love you feel for your child will blow you away. And it only gets stronger with time.

I used to think it was a jerk thing to say that you won't understand until it happens, but now I think it's honestly one of life's greatest and most satisfying surprises. I don't think it means that we can't love with our whole heart, or value others, or feel intensity about another person. I think it's its own special category of emotion.

But I do think that many moms tend to wear their embattled hearts as a badge of honor. And they tend to make other people–maybe even especially expecting moms–feel like motherhood is a barrage of hard and awful stuff. You hear them say, "Oh, you had a night of bad sleep? Wait until you have kids!" It's not helpful, and it's not even entirely true. We don't need to be martyrs. We can respect everyone's experiences. And, I think that you can enjoy the hell out of motherhood. It's so much more fun than I expected, and I was pretty sure I was going to like being a mom. Not everything is awful and hard. No question, some of it is hard, but the rewards are so sweet.

The old-school dictionary characterization of a "supermom" is a woman who raises a child or children all while taking care of a home and also having a full-time job. It that your definition of a "supermom"?

Nope. I think every mom who puts her heart and soul into what's she's doing is a supermom. We all have our talents and strengths, and our families are all so different that to put only one category of mom into that word feels really reductive. Moms who stay home full time have a limitless kind of patience I can only aspire to, for example. Working moms have to juggle between professional and family and personal selves. But all moms don't get enough time to themselves, even with loving and doting spouses or partners. To pour that much love and to prioritize that way, to me, is pretty super.

How do you use your alone time?

I take a long, hot shower. Or read a magazine. I might steal a few moments on the phone with my best friend. And I will never give up my regular appointment to get my hair colored.

How do you and your husband find time to focus on each other with such hectic schedules?

We both run our own businesses from home, and we're both fairly intense people. It's hard for us sometimes, to be honest. We're together a lot since we share an office, but a lot of our together time is work or parenting. And then we're exhausted at the end of the day. But we both love television-and watch and discuss a lot of our favorite shows together after Ruby goes to bed. We go see our favorite bands when they have shows in town. This summer, we ate lunch together outside when it was nice. We try to steal moments here and there, and keep a good sense of humor otherwise.

What do you enjoy most about being a mother?

I was so fortunate to be raised by an extraordinary mother. I was a very anxious and fearful child and I always felt so safe with my mom. She didn't judge, and she was so supportive. I've come to find that I love being Ruby's safe harbor. I hope she always sees me as such. But honestly, I love being a mom altogether. I love giggling with her, I love watching her skills explode, I love snuggling up with a good book, and I love that when she is scared, sad, or needing reassurance that I can provide that, too.

How has your life changed?
How hasn't it? I quit my fairly high-profile job to go freelance and have more flexibility. My patience-never a strength-has gotten a good workout. The moment Ruby arrived, my priority list completely rearranged. And I think sometimes people perceive that as a bad thing. But I think it's made me a better person. A less-organized, more sleep-deprived, and maybe a less-social person, but a better person nonetheless.

What percentage do you think parenting has on the overall outcome of a child's life? Why?
Hmm. Nature or nurture, right? I think my job as a parent is to get to know Ruby as she unfolds, then help her enrich that. I hope I can keep my control out of it and let her become herself. As she does, I hope I can see what she needs and what I can teach her-how to handle conflict, how to manage emotions, how to analyze a book's message, how to bake cookies, whatever it is-to help her navigate the life she wants and the life she deserves.

What are your thoughts on young children using electronic devices, such as iPads?
I try to really limit Ruby's exposure to electronic devices, since she's not even two. But I don't want to do anything too iron-fisted. I don't want to overlook an opportunity or make it more appealing by denying something, whether it's technol-

ogy or some band's music or whatever. I hope I can teach her how to make technology her friend and to use it for good.

What parenting technique do you use that your mother/father used?

When I read *Bringing Up Bébé*, a book written by an American journalist living in France and exploring why French children are so different from American children, I realized that my parents had inadvertently often parented like the French. They were consistent, and they were the bosses. But they were loving and kind and let me be who I was. I hope I can do the same for Ruby. I think the world of my parents.

Does being a mother define you? Why or why not?

It's not the only thing that defines me. I'm a lot of other things, too: Wife, friend, sister, writer, cheese fanatic, worrier. But I would say that in this stage of my life, it's the most important thing about me. I spend all my waking hours doing something in service of my daughter. I work because I love to write, but I also do so to afford a good life for her. Ruby informs every decision I make. And she brings out the best in me. I really believe that.

If you could wish one thing for your daughter in this lifetime, what would it be?

Only one thing? Man...I wish for her a life where she feels

armed with the smarts and the confidence and love to take on the world. We can't control what goes on around us, but we can control how we react, and what we are affected by, and how to improve. Basically, I hope she believes in herself as much as I believe in her.

On crazy days, how do you stay sane?

Sometimes I have a good cry. Sometimes I have a good laugh. It really depends on the amount of crazy. A call to a friend or my mom. A long, hot shower. Reminding myself that whatever it is that is making me crazy, will it matter in five minutes? Five years? Try to keep things in perspective. I also have been known to rant about the state of America on particularly terrible days. I also belong to a great moms group on Facebook where we can talk about anything.

Do you consider yourself a mommy blogger/writer? Why or why not?

Anything that is qualified by "mommy" kind of bugs me. "Mompreneur" really gets me. You never hear "Dadpreneur!" But I literally write for a blog geared toward mamas. So yes, I do *do* that. But I do a lot of other things too. I coordinate editorial calendars. I write about travel, education, fashion, wellness, and home décor. I am a politics junkie. Again, being a mom really defines this stage of my life, but it's not the whole of me.

What's your favorite quote?

"Our deepest fear is not that we are inadequate. Our deepest fear is that we are powerful beyond measure. It is our light, not our darkness that most frightens us. We ask ourselves, 'Who am I to be brilliant, gorgeous, talented and fabulous?' Actually, who are you *not* to be? You are a child of God. Your playing small does not serve the world. There is nothing enlightened about shrinking so that other people will not feel insecure around you. We are all meant to shine, as children do. We were born to make manifest the glory of God that is within us. It is not just in some of us; it is in everyone and as we let our own light shine, we unconsciously give others permission to do the same. As we are liberated from our own fear, our presence automatically liberates others."
– Marianne Williamson

Introspection

Write down five reasons why you love being a mother:

What are three ways that you connect with your children?

List a few ways that you spend quality time with your children:

What has been your favorite memory (as a mother) to date?

List three of your best parenting strengths:

Write down three ways that you replenish your own energy and resources:

Name five people who support you as a mother and a way that you can express your gratitude for them:

If your children were to find this workbook someday, what would you want them to know?

Suggested Resources

Books:

The Secrets of Happy Families by Bruce Feiler

Carry On, Warrior: The Power of Embracing Your Messy, Beautiful Life by Glennon Doyle Melton

Websites:
- scarymommy.com
- coffeeandcrumbs.net

Apps:
- Cozi
- Evernote

Katie Dohman's info:
- Website: katiedohman.contently.com
- Twitter: @katiedohman

Thoughts

"Relationships should be a two-way street."

- Unknown

Interdependency + {Relationships}

The most rewarding, yet complex, relationship that you can have is one with another human being.

The saying "it's not you, it's me" is complete rubbish. It takes two people to make or break a relationship. Accountability, flexibility and honesty are just a few hallmarks that help foster a healthy and loving relationship.

This chapter is dedicated to retaining, reconnecting, repairing, or releasing relationships. It can be applied to a variety of relationships–significant others, mothers, friends, or co-workers.

First, it's important to know if the relationship is codependent or interdependent.

Mental Health America defines codependency as an *"emotional and behavioral condition that affects an individual's ability to have a healthy, mutually satisfying relationship.*"[1] It is also known as "relationship addiction" because people with codependency often form or maintain relationships that are one-sided, emotionally destructive and/or abusive.

I was a codependent and a love addict for years. Friends and family would mention my (unhealthy and unsolicited) need to fix others or play the martyr. I just ignored them, thinking it's *just because I care so much.* But it wasn't until this past year, and after many failed relationships with men, that I realized I was the mayor of Codependent County.

When I read the list of characteristics of codependents, I felt weirdly validated and relieved. I was finally able to identify behaviors in myself and others and why some relationships didn't work or weren't working. There is such a thing as healthy codependency. It's just being able to know and live the difference.

Jo-Ann Svensson, a body/mind therapist, says, "*With codependence, there is an energy loss for at least one of the participants. In interdependence, there is energy gain (or at least neutrality) for all persons involved. Codependent people usually look to someone else to be their source of validation, acceptance or*

---

1. "Co-Dependency." *mentalhealthamerica.net.* © Mental Health America. November 20, 2014.

safety. An interdependent person looks within first and views themselves as whole and balanced, and welcomes external sources as a healthy complement to life."[2]

With either therapy, self-education, positive self-talk and exercises, or all of the above, one can move from codependency into a healthier dynamic of interdependency.

I don't like to use the words "detox" or "toxic" when it comes to evaluating relationships. The goal here is to create as many interdependent relationships in our lives as possible by retaining, reconnecting, repairing, or releasing.

Releasing doesn't have to mean writing someone off—it just might mean letting them go for now.

2. Jo-Ann Svensson. "Interdependence vs Codependence." *theinterdependentlife.blogspot*.com

Retain

When we are retaining a relationship, we are actively nurturing it. We often take for granted the relationships that are *working* for us, which is a normal response to stability. But even the best relationships need attention and to be reaffirmed.

Introspection

List the five most meaningful relationships that you're in right now and why:

WHO?   WHY?

1.

2.

3.

4.

5.

———————————— 💭 ————————————

Think of the last time that you did something out of the ordinary for each person. What did you do or say?

Name one person that you will do something out of the ordinary for this week. What will you do? What day will you do it?

Reconnect

Our lives are so busy and it seems impossible to keep up with friends and family members. When too much time has passed, it makes us feel that we can't reach out. But think about it, when a friend calls you up out of the blue and says, "Hey! I miss you! Let's catch up!" do you hang up on them? Well, unless you're a bitch, the answer is no you don't. You match their excitement and energy, with, "I'm so glad you called/texted/left a message. I've missed you too!"

Introspection

List three people that you've fallen out of touch with:

How would you like to reach out to them?

What is a practice that you can put into motion to stay in touch with friends and family?

Repair

Sometimes misunderstandings and hurt feelings can cause rifts in relationships with someone that you care about. This not only takes an emotional toll, but a physical one as well. Scientists have found that negative social interactions can lead to increased inflammation, which may in turn cause a host of illnesses, from cancer to heart disease and high blood pressure.

It's time to put the past in the past and accept that in order to repair, you will need to be the person who reaches out. You don't have to admit fault, but you can express that you're sorry that words and/or actions have led you to this point in your relationship. (Do accept some responsibility.)

Introspection

List a few people that you'd like to repair + reconnect with and why:

WHO?   WHY?

1.

2.

3.

4.

5.

interdependency + {relationships}

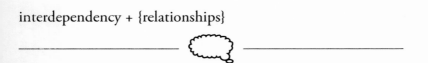

What are you going to say or do when you reach out to them?
What day will you do it?

How can you prevent future misunderstandings with the
people in your life?

Release

"Some people believe holding on and hanging in there are signs of great strength. However, there are times when it takes much more strength to know when to let go and then do it."
- Ann Landers

We often find ourselves in relationships that we know aren't working for us, but we have done nothing about it. Perhaps this non-action and complacency stems from fear, apathy, or just because it's become a part of your existence for so long that the pain and conflict feels normal.

Introspection

Think about the people in your life who are not healthy for your overall growth as a person. Who are these people?

Why are you in conflict with them?

How are you going to release them? When?

Suggested Resources

Books:

Daring Greatly: How the Courage to Be Vulnerable Transforms the Way We Live, Love, Parent, and Lead by Brené Brown

The 5 Love Languages: The Secret to Love That Lasts by Gary D Chapman

Websites:

- theinterdependentlife.blogspot.com
- loveandlifetoolbox.com

Apps:

- More Language of Letting Go
- RelationTips

*"Success is living a life
that is 100% authentic."*

- Suzanne LeRoux

Career + {Success}

My career began when Head First Salon called and asked if I'd like to be their receptionist. I was 15 at the time and didn't have a driver's license yet. I asked Jan, the owner of the salon, to hold on the line while I asked my parents if I could accept the job. They agreed and I've been in the beauty industry ever since.

Early in my career I defined success as a big title and big paycheck. I was always chasing the carrot, quitting jobs if they weren't advancing me quickly enough.

I purchased my first Louis Vuitton handbag at age 22, and my first BMW five years later. I had high hopes of climbing my way to the top of the corporate ladder so I could buy more designer handbags and German cars, and tell everyone that I was some high-profiled, very important executive.

But then I got bored of my desk job and at the age of 30, I started my own company and everything changed. I no longer had the steady income to afford a BMW. I had the business cards that read "owner" but no one had heard of my company or knew who I was. I'd given up a promising corporate career to become a starving makeup artist.

And guess what? It was a fit. I loved creating something from nothing and watching it grow. I didn't make a ton of money, but I didn't care. I was in my creative element.

Success was no longer about the job title and money. Instead, it had everything to do with how challenged and fulfilled I was in my career.

Don't get me wrong: there were plenty of roadblocks along the way. When I sold my business, the deal blew up in my face. I went from having a thriving company (in terms of the amount of business it generated, awards and its reputation) to being in a financial crisis and a solo artist without a team. Those were some dark hours in my life. I was pushing on one button and it was called *self-destruct*.

My turning point was inspired by this quote:
"A setback is a setup for a comeback."- Unknown

With the help of friends and colleagues, I was able to pull myself up by my bootstraps and start over. And once again, my definition of success evolved.

Success was less about the job itself and more about who I was becoming and what I could contribute. I had purpose.

I began mentoring other makeup artists, started a training center for aspiring artists, launched a beauty wellness brand (Beauty PhD), and began working with women with cancer.

The Oxford dictionaries defines success as, "the attainment of popularity or profit, or a person or thing that achieves desired aims or attains prosperity."[1]

It's no wonder why we're conditioned to look at success in a one-dimensional way. The dictionary doesn't list the subjective elements of success like enjoyment of work, pride in accomplishments, and a happy marriage. Instead we are influenced by our ego and seek out objective factors like salary and awards.

This doesn't mean we shouldn't set objective goals for ourselves. Goals are good! Go ahead, buy that Mercedes. But, take into consideration that objective factors often leave us feeling dissatisfied and unfulfilled.

It's time for us to create our own definition of success.

---

1. "Success." *oxforddictionaries.com.* © 2014 Oxford University Press.

Introspection

Define success:

On scale from 1-10 how successful in work and life are you?
(1 being oops, not at all and 10 being pretty darn successful)

What could you do to increase your success?

Who in your life do you consider a successful person? Why?

Describe a time when you felt successful:

Suggested Resources

Books:

The Seven Spiritual Laws of Success: A Practical Guide to the Fulfillment of Your Dreams by Deepak Chopra

The Diamond Cutter: The Buddha on Managing Your Business and Your Life by Geshe Michael Roach

Websites:
- oprah.com
- becomingminimalist.com

Apps:
- Eckhart Tolle–Discovering Your True Purpose
- Omvana–Meditation for everyone

Thoughts

"Live as if your were to die tomorrow. Learn as if you were to live forever."

— Gandhi

Education + {Learning}

I dreamed of becoming a writer since I was a child. So naturally, I thought I'd study journalism at the University of Minnesota. Then I took my first journalism class and received a C. Not even a C+. A horribly ugly C was permanently burned onto my transcript. I was shocked, bewildered, and devastated. I felt like a fraud. I felt like I let everyone who had ever supported me as a writer-my family, my friends, and my teachers-and myself down. I felt like I failed. And it wasn't only a failure in a single course—it was a failure of a dream.

After a bit of soul searching, I dropped out of college and enrolled at the Aveda Institute. By that time, I had been working in a salon for five years, so it seemed logical to pursue an industry in which I was comfortable and familiar. While working at a salon in Beverly Hills, California, I started taking classes again from the University of Minnesota. The Internet was still new, so online courses weren't an option yet.

I had to mail in my assignments. Over the years, I continued taking courses whenever my career and family life would allow.

Then, finally, came the day I walked across a stage to accept my diploma. When I saw my name on the commencement program, I was both proud and amused. So what if it took me 20 years to get my undergraduate degree? I didn't really need it, but come hell or high water, I was determined to finish it.

Now I am enrolled in a Masters in Integrative Health and Wellness program. What can I say? I am a life-long student. I like everything about being a student. I like having assignments, expanding my mind and getting graded on my work. The biggest reason that I continue to seek out more education is to keep my brain stimulated. I thrive off of new information and knowledge. It makes me feel awake and alive.

In the *Life Magazine* article, "Building a Better Brain," writer Daniel Golden states, "Evidence is accumulating that the brain works a lot like a muscle—the harder you use it, the more it grows."[1]

In his research, Golden found that the brain has a remarkable capacity to change and grow, even into old age, and that

---

1. Golden, Daniel. "Building a Better Brain." *Life Magazine*. July, 1994: page 62. Magazine print.

individuals have some control over how healthy and alert their brains remain as the years go by.

In other words, keep learning and our brains will grow.

If we stop stimulating our brains, the synapses between neurons that contain our memories and give us our reasoning powers are likely being wiped out as we get older.

Yikes! Let's not let that happen, right?

I am not suggesting that you must enroll at a university. Courses and degree programs can get expensive. I am encouraging you to seek out learning opportunities that will keep your brain stimulated and engaged. Continued education helps us adapt to change, find meaning in our lives and makes us active participants in life. Exercising the brain can be as simple as taking a cooking class, taking up crossword puzzles or, for a greater challenge, learning a new language.

Introspection

List three things you're currently doing to stimulate your brain:

List three things you'd like to learn about and why:

What were three of your favorite subjects in school and why?

If you had the time and money, what advanced degree would you pursue? Why?

Suggested Resources

Books:

Grain Brain: The Surprising Truth about Wheat, Carbs, and Sugar–Your Brain's Silent Killers by David Perlmutter

Why Isn't My Brain Working?: A Revolutionary Understanding of Brain Decline and Effective Strategies to Recover Your Brain's Health by Dr. Datis Kharrazian

Websites:

- Check out your local community education
- britannica.com

Apps:

- Duolingo
- Quizup

Thoughts

*"Do it with passion
or not at all."*

- Unknown

Projects + {Passions}

I used to think that it was important, if not crucial, to be passionate about your career. But realistically, not everyone is going to have a love affair with their 9-5 job. When I talk to clients who are eager to quit their job in pursuit of one that would make them happier, I ask them a series a questions such as:

Are your company's values aligned with your own?
Have you completely checked out?
Are you losing sleep because of your job?
Are you bored? Feeling stagnate?

This helps assess if they are willing to give up certain aspects of the job, like tenure and stability, for a job that might be more fulfilling. *Might* is the operative word here.

Consider this saying: "*You may think the grass is greener, but if you water your own grass it would be just as green.*" Sometimes it's not the job you need to quit, but it's a deeper calling to discover passions and pursuing projects outside of your career.

Using the word "project" can sound like work, especially since it's used in the workplace and is often associated with deadlines, expectations, and micromanagement. Do you remember working on a science or an art project in grade school? Remember the wonder and excitement that came with creating something with our own hands and mind? When did we stop doing projects? It was probably somewhere between college age and into adulthood when time became limited and it was more important to pay the bills and raise a family.

While my career keeps me busy, I still like to carve out time to do projects and hobbies that relax me, like baking or playing piano. I also like to do fairly mindless activities, like drinking wine. Wait, that's not a project?

It's time for you to put your creative cap on, pour yourself a glass of wine, and start a project, yo!

Stephany Wieland of *Making It With Stephany* is a woman who rocks her creative cap. Her DIY channel on YouTube is informative, arming you with all you need for a certain project. Her projects are easy, fun and useful. And bonus! Stephany is HILARIOUS. Yes, all caps HILARIOUS.

Q + A
with Stephany Wieland

You've recently created a website and YouTube channel that demonstrates easy and modern DIY projects. What inspired you to share it with the masses opposed to just the ladies in your neighborhood?

I was never impressed with most store-bought products. Remember how much tastier your mom's homemade cookies were over some packaged crap? That is how I started looking at everything in life. Why bother wasting time on mediocre things when I could make WAY better stuff?

I started customizing whatever I could, be it food, clothes, furniture, you name it. If I wasn't happy with what was offered at the store, I started replacing it with my own, improved versions. I now know how to make/do/fix/execute a lot of baking/sewing/life/art/home decor/building/crafting/gardening things.

Then, my friends would call me over the years and ask me how to make or do something, or what was the secret ingredient in some recipe I had made. It then became obvious that I needed to share my know-it-all-ness with the masses. And what better way to do it than broadcasting my face all over the Internet?!

You seem to be having fun with *Making It*. Would you say this has been a fulfilling/meaningful experience?
Creating the videos is a riot! I am making all of the decisions, like the insane, entrepreneurial control freak that I am. I get to plan specific projects that I enjoy doing, research and write up the episodes, and say boneheaded things to make them funny and entertaining to watch.

The most challenging part for me is the episode's presentation. Since I do the editing as well, I want them to be the best they can be. I have no formal training in video editing, so I do a lot of cutting, then beg my editor friends for feedback. Once everything is perfect, I upload and pray that everyone likes them as much as I do.

There is nothing more terrifying than posting videos of yourself and inviting everyone you know to watch. If they suck, it's all on me. But if they're good, I get to own that, too.

Do you think it's important for people to have interests and hobbies outside of work and family?
Totally! When I get bored with life or stressed from work,

making new things is my outlet. And from experimenting with these new interests, I develop new skills and become a more interesting human being. I'm a great guest at dinner parties.

Do you think there are more or less hobbies to do now because of technology? How has technology served as a vehicle to inspire more interests?

The Internet is fulfilling its destiny for providing instant gratification. If you have a DIY question, or you want to know how something is made, you go straight to the inter-webs. Ten years ago, I was still watching Martha Stewart for craft ideas that were months old. I did the same thing with magazines. Now, if I want to make something, I get on the computer, look up my project, buy the supplies and watch a YouTube video on how to do it all in an afternoon.

What are you feelings on Pinterest and Etsy?

Sites like Pinterest and Etsy are great inspiration and idea starters. I love the idea of Pinterest and how it catalogs your Internet finds. I think it gets the creative juices flowing in a lot of people who didn't consider making things before. And once you get into making things it really opens the door to a new, custom world.

And with Etsy, it's refreshing to see that there are makers out there and that people are ready to buy something handmade over running to Target and getting the generic version. Handmade has so much personality to it. I have a hard time saying no to anything homemade.

When you hear someone has "passions," what does that mean to you? Would you consider *Making It* a passion?
Making It With Stephany didn't start out as a passion. It was more of a thought like, "Hmm, what would happen if I started making funny videos about crafty things I know how to do?"

It was definitely an experiment that I became obsessed with the instant I finished editing the first video. I'm super competitive in everything I do, so if I start something and it's not perfect, you better know that I am coming right back at it 100 times harder.

When I feel passionate about something, I absorb as much information on the subject as I can, practice, then master it. The tricky thing about mastering your passion is that you have to keep your mind fresh with ideas. Otherwise you get bored. Which can lead to discovering a new passion.

Some say that DIY projects are cathartic and empowering. Would you agree with this?

Hell yes! Using a circular saw and a nail gun is a fantastic stress reliever! After seeing a finished product that you made with your own hands, you might get a little *swank* in your step. And it's okay because you are a *maker* now.

What do you think holds people back from trying new things? How do they overcome this?

It takes practice. I think people are afraid to step outside of their box, their *safeness*, if you will. They don't want people to look at them as different. On the same token, people are drawn to interesting and unique things.

But damn, that is where you have fun in life! I love taking risks, in life and work. If you don't have that in you naturally, I can see it being hard to start, but I don't see how standing out in a crowd is a bad thing? Boring is boring!

What is your favorite quote?

I love this Albert Einstein quote I came across a few years ago: "I have no special talent. I am only passionately curious."

I love learning as much as I can about subjects that interest me. When I want to learn about something new, I am pretty obsessive-compulsive about it, until I know as much as I can. Then I move on to the next idea.

What else do we need to know about why projects are cool? Customizing your life is amazing! It opens the doors to so many new things. Your friends will soon be asking you where you got all of your awesome handmade things, then you drop a craft bomb on them by saying casually, "Oh, I made it. No big deal."

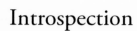

Introspection

On a scale from 1-10, how passionate are you about the things that you're doing right now? (1 being that you feel dead inside and 10 being that you are very passionate in all areas of your life)

What can you do to increase the amount of passion in your life?

Write down three activities outside of your work that you enjoy and why:

Write down three activities that you liked to do in your childhood. Why do you think you enjoyed them?

What is one hobby or project that you'd like to explore this year?

Think of a person that you could get involved in a hobby or project with you. Why do you think that person would also enjoy it?

Would you sell or donate your project? If yes, where would you do this? (Etsy, Artfire, local shops, etc.) If you'd donate, what organization would you donate to?

Suggested Resources

Books:

Get a Hobby!: 101 All-Consuming Diversions for Any Lifestyle by Tina Barseghian

The Element: How Finding Your Passion Changes Everything by Ken Robinson

Websites:
- abeautifulmess.com
- hobbies.meetup.com

Apps:
- Craftgawker
- DIY Lifestyle Magazine

Stephany Wieland's info:
- Website: makingitwithstephany.com
- Facebook: facebook.com/makingitwithstephany
- Twitter: @makeitwithsteph
- Instagram: @makingitwithstephany
- Pinterest: pinterest.com/makingitwithstephany

projects + {passions}

Thoughts

*"All those who travel
are not lost."*

- J.R.R. Tolkien

Travel + {Exploration}

In recent years I've taken some trips by myself that have helped me gain perspective and get back to my center.

Last year I took a trip to St. Thomas, in the US Virgin Islands. I was supposed to go with a boyfriend, but we broke up just weeks before and I decided to go by myself. I was turning 37 years old on the trip, and I wanted to spend it alone. Not because I wanted to isolate myself, but because I had been feeling out of control, and I knew spending quality time with myself would get me back in balance.

I arrived at my "guest house" (or, as some call it, a hostel) and was greeted by Sonny, the caretaker, who became my unofficial driver for the week. He drove me to places off the beaten path and shared the story of his life with me. He had run away to St. Thomas as a young boy and has been a fixture on the island ever since. He took me to a street dance on my birthday, where the locals fed me johnny cakes and homemade rum. I danced to reggae that blared from parked vans. I thought, *stay in this moment Julie, savor it.*

The day after my birthday I decided to take a sailing lesson on the island of St. John. Ike, the instructor, and I ventured off to sea on a Hobie Cat sailboat. When we got out of the bay into the open water, I started to have a small panic attack.

What am I doing on this tiny raft? I'm not a great swimmer. What if the boat capsizes? No one knows I'm out here.

I tried to hide my fear from Ike by smiling at him every now and then, but I was still thinking, *I'm going to die out here!*

I began to feel sick from the boat's motion. We sailed to the closest beach and Ike encouraged me to swim, stating it would ease my stomach. I dove into the water and my motion sickness disappeared immediately. Ike and I talked and swam for a good portion of the afternoon. He told me about his life in the Navy and how he had made a life decision to leave the military and explore the world by boat. Ike lives moment to moment. He said, "As long as I have my guitar, my sailboat and my surfboard, that's all I need in life." Our conversation had a profound effect on me. It jump-started my process of letting go of the past and focusing on the present.

My time in the US Virgin Islands makes me think of this quote:

"Sometimes people come into your life and you know right away that they were meant to be there, to serve some sort of purpose, teach you a lesson, or to help you figure out who you are or who you want to become." – Unknown

It's no secret that I have a full-on addiction to traveling. Traveling just makes me, well, happy. So it comes as no surprise that a recent study about the physical, cognitive and social benefits of travel revealed that women who vacation often are less likely to have heart failure, have significantly less stress and are able to ward off depression.

The bottom line: traveling keeps us happy and healthy.

I get it though. Not everyone has the time or the means to travel. But travel doesn't have to be about getting on a plane and going to an island in the Caribbean. Travel can mean simply getting out of our comfort zone to experience something new and different. Like exploring local parks, lakes, hell, even Target stores.

The idea is to go somewhere, anywhere that makes us take in a deep breath and slow down.

Travel photographer Laura Ivanova explores the world with wild abandon. With a camera in one hand and bottle of water in the other, she fearlessly immerses herself in local culture, snapping stunning, poignant photographs and soaking in the once-in-a-lifetime experiences.

Q + A
with Laura Ivanova

How or why do you think travel and exploration changes a person (for the better)?

I believe one of the best ways to grow is to put yourself out there, step out of your comfort zone, and take risks. This applies to everything–life, business, and travel. One of the biggest risks I've taken in my life (maybe the very biggest) is leaving a comfortable full-time job to pursue my dream of running my own business. At the time, like everyone, I had responsibilities–a mortgage, a spouse who had recently gone back to school and was a full-time student, loan debt from college, and I was absolutely terrified to leave the security of a steady paycheck. The risk was great, but so was the reward. Travel is also about taking a risk. Often times it's stepping into the unknown. But, it enriches our lives. It's a change from the ordinary. It's fun and exciting. It gives us great memories and stories to share with others or to experience just for ourselves.

Besides time and money, why do you think people are afraid to travel? How can they overcome these fears?

This question stumped me a bit because I can only speak from personal experience. So I reached out to friends and family to ask them what prohibits them from traveling. Far and away, the number one response was children.

I also believe that people don't travel out of fear–perhaps fear of the journey itself, fear of leaving the comforts of home, fear of danger or dangerous places. Life just gets in the way. A friend of mine referred to it as the "someday" factor. We get caught up in the everyday of life and it's easy to put off that dream trip.

Of course, these are all legitimate factors and not really something that can be overcome. I think if a person has a strong desire to travel (or do anything!), they'll make it a priority in their lives. People often ask me how I can travel so much, or how I can afford it, and my answer is that I've made sacrifices in other areas of my life. My husband and I choose to live in a small home. (We're talking 850 square feet!) We choose to drive older cars and not have car loans. We have a roommate to help pay our mortgage. All of these things allow us greater flexibility financially. My advice is if you want to travel, just do it! Be smart financially, but beyond that, you have to take risks!

What are five of your best travel tips?

1. Pack light! It's tough, but so worth it. No one wants to roll a big ol' bag around the cobblestone streets of Europe, up and down flights of stairs to the Metro, or across train platforms. Or even worse, have lost luggage and be without all your belongings for a few (or more) days! Yikes!

My worst travel experiences involve lost luggage. Take-away: carry on! It's not as hard as you think. I'm writing this on a flight from Moscow to New York City and I spent the last month (spanning four countries in two continents with a variety of weather conditions) living out of a carry-on. And, truth be told, I could've left many clothing items behind.

Keep it simple. Plan to hand wash clothing. Skip the heels (in most scenarios) and stick with comfortable yet stylish street shoes, hiking/running shoes if needed, and a pair of broken-in and trusty ballet flats. I stick with neutral clothing pieces that can be worn in a variety of ways, like dark denim, black leggings, a black blouse, a striped tee, a grey tee, and a couple versatile blazers that can go from day to night. I pack one quick-dry workout/hiking/lazy outfit that I can quickly hand wash after every use and that will dry overnight. And wear your biggest and bulkiest items on the plane.

2. Be open-minded. It can be tough to leave your precon-ceived notions behind, but try. Don't assume you know what you're getting yourself into. Be open to new experiences, meeting new people and trying new things. It's good to plan and do research, but even if you have an itinerary, be flexible. If the weather sucks, who cares? You'll probably have limited time at your destination, so try to enjoy every second and make the most of your precious adventure.

3. Consider the off-season. (But be especially mindful of #2, as off-season can sometimes equate to less ideal weather!) Off-season can mean lower airfare, fewer crowds, and deals on accommodations. One of my favorite little secrets is Kayak Explorer (kayak.com/explore). You can input your departure city, price cap, and desired departure date range and see airfare costs to destinations around the world on a map.

For my last birthday, I took a spur-of-the-moment solo trip to Ireland because I found an absolute airfare steal on Kayak Explorer. I bought the ticket on a Thursday, left on Sunday, and woke up on Monday in Dublin on my 32nd birthday, with a rental car and a week at my disposal to explore the country. I hadn't booked any accommodations; I just planned to go wherever the road took me.

Going to Ireland in December can be a little risky, as it is usually chilly and rainy, but I got lucky with six amazing days (and only one rainy day). And I saved a fortune.

4. Learn the language. Try to learn a few key phrases of the language of the place you're visiting. *"Hi.", "Do you speak English?", "Where's the toilet?", "Thank you.", "Excuse me."* These terms will likely come in handy. People will appreciate it greatly and it's so much kinder than expecting everyone to speak your language and cater to you.

5. Don't be afraid to travel alone. As mentioned above, I think one of the reasons people don't travel is because they have no one to go with. Why let that stop you? I have traveled extensively–solo, with my husband, with my best friend, with one friend, with groups of friends, with colleagues. The more I travel, and the older I get, the more I realize my preferences. We all have our preferences, but be open minded and don't be afraid to try traveling differently. I happen to love traveling alone, as I'm very independent. I can do exactly as I please, and I enjoy time to myself. I don't mind eating alone and I find I am much more receptive to meeting new people and carrying on a conservation when I'm not with people who I already know. I also find that people find me more approachable when I'm alone. My favorite travel memories involve meeting locals, and I think they're more likely to interact with you if you're alone.

Describe your most transformative travel moment.

I have a really poignant memory of a trip to Thailand. I was traveling with my husband and two friends. We had spent a busy few days in Bangkok before flying out to Krabi to enjoy the serene beaches. We checked into our hotel in the late afternoon and had some time to make our way to the beach to enjoy the sunset.

This trip happened several years ago, so I don't remember specific details, but somehow I ended up on my own on this beautiful beach. The sun had dipped below the horizon and all of these crabs began to emerge from the sand. The tide was really low at this point, so I could see hundreds of thousands of these little creatures.

The sky had turned a shade of dusky blue that I had never seen before. It was so peaceful. It was also a time in my life when I had just begun practicing yoga, so that solitude with the quiet longtail boats that dotted the shore, felt like a really poignant moment for me. It was a moment that I will remember forever. To this day, whenever I'm wrapping up a yoga practice and laying the final pose of *savasana*, I transport back to that beach. It's funny how certain seemingly insignificant moments have stayed with me.

Why is it important to explore, even if it's just a few miles down the road?
I think exploration and adventure adds excitement to my life. It helps me avoid the rut of floating through the days. It makes me appreciate where I live and realize that I'm lucky to call my home "home."

Exploration doesn't have to be exotic. When I was younger, I constantly desired to see the furthest reaches of the Earth—and I still do—but I have also come to realize that there is so much beauty in our own backyards. Something as simple as an overnight trip can recharge my creativity and energy. I also think the anticipation of exploration can be as exciting as the trip itself. Planning trips and daydreaming is a hobby for me. I look forward to this part of the adventure too.

Introspection

List three local places that you'd like to explore and the dates that you plan to:

Name three places that you'd like to travel to and specify the dates that you plan to travel there:

What are three ways you can get out of your everyday routine?

What are some of your fears about traveling? How will you overcome them?

Name a movie that inspires you to travel. Why does it have that effect on you?

travel+ {exploration}

Think of a trip that you'd like to take by yourself. Where would you go and what would you do?

travel+ {exploration}

Write a story about a trip that influenced your life:

Suggested Resources

Books:

Off the Beaten Path: A Travel Guide to More Than 1000 Scenic and Interesting Places Still Uncrowded and Inviting
by Reader's Digest

Journeys of a Lifetime: 500 of the World's Greatest Trips
by National Geographic

Websites:
- fathomaway.com
- tripadvisor.com

Apps:
- Tripit
- Scout

Laura Ivanova's info:
- Websites: lauraivanova.com, traveler.lauraivanova.com
- Facebook: facebook.com/lauraivanovaphotography
- Twitter: @lauraivanova
- Instagram: @lauraivanova
- Pinterest: pinterest.com/lauraivanovaphotography

"When you do things from your soul, people really dig that shit."

- Unknown

Community + {Social Connectedness}

Amber, Noah, Kevin, Carrie and Karen are the names of the kids I used to play with in my neighborhood as a child. Somehow, with our young minds, we planned out where we were going to meet, what we were going to do and who was going to be in charge. Playing with my neighborhood "gang" is the earliest memory I have of belonging to a community.

It's human nature to desire a sense of belonging, acceptance and connection with others. It's built into our DNA. It's what keeps our species thriving.

Research scientist, Emma Seppala, Ph.D., says, "social connection improves physical health and mental and emotional well-being."[1]

Fostering personal relationships with family, friends and significant others plays an important role in social connected-

1. Seppala, Emma, Ph.D. "Connectedness & Health: The Science of Social Connection INFOGRAPHIC." *emmaseppala.com*. April 11, 2014.

ness, as does involvement in groups such as sports teams, office culture, spiritual and religious organizations, and social media groups. It's in building these mini- and mega-communities that we cultivate a sense of belonging and find more meaning in our lives.

In Dan Buettner's book, *The Blue Zones: Lessons for Living Longer From the People Who've Lived the Longest*, he writes about areas of the world where people have lived measurably better than in other countries.

I was especially moved by Buettner's study of the Blue Zone in Okinawa, Japan. The people of Okinawa have created social networks called Moais. Groups of children from a young age pledge their support and companionship. They stay within these groups their entire life.

Perhaps Amber, Noah, Kevin, Carrie, Karen, and I would have created a Moai had we not been a product of urbanization. It's simply not in our American culture to operate as a group. However, the pendulum is beginning to swing as people like Dan Buettner are waking us up to the benefits of social connectedness and the impact it makes on our whole-body health.

community + {social connectedness}

One outstanding community builder and social connector is Mary Pokluda, founder of Bumblebee Personal Assistants. Mary has a wildly successful lifestyle business. Beyond her own "hive" of employees, she has built an extensive community of people from all backgrounds. She is an active member of many organizations and has earned a Connector Award from Women In Networking. Mary supports a number of charities, and her own non-profit will launch in the coming year.

Q + A
with Mary Pokluda

Is there a difference between networking and connecting?
Networking is working a room to find people that have a positive attitude, can align with your business and are looking to connect with others to potentially collaborate on any level.

Connecting happens when people meet independently and then find that their values, morals and ethics align. After that, they connect on a potential partner level for business, become colleagues, resources, or mentors.

Why do you think tight knit communities are the happiest on Earth?
Everyone working toward the same goal means that people are unified, working together, and have the same vision. It creates positivity and like-minded energy.

How can shy or introverted individuals reach out and become part of a community?
Try selecting events that really resonate with them, which will help ease the stress of stepping out. Also, having a "wing-man" helps because each person will be able to speak to the

others' attributes, as it's easier to speak of other successes and accomplishments versus our own.

Rather than attending large networking events, try reaching out to specific individuals for a one-on-one connection. It can also ease tension to start out on the phone, where you can prepare a set of questions. It may feel awkward at first to have a script, but it can help give you confidence to have a plan for what you want to say. Making those sorts of appointments also allow you to set a start and stop time that can help structure what might feel like ambiguous social interaction.

The important thing to remember about becoming a member of the community is to be genuine. Networking may seem like you're being insincere, because you are trying to "get" something from others. But community members help each other, and there is nothing wrong with that.

Are social networks (Facebook, Instagram, Twitter) real communities?
We are as successful as the people we surround ourselves with, so if our social networks are filled with positive, giving, contributing followers, then the network truly is a "real community."

What are the pros and cons of social networks?

Pros: Connecting with a community on a real-time basis allows us to tap into a network that will give immediate response, feedback, opportunities, help, and support even when they're not within arm's reach.

Cons: People forget that there are real people on the other side of their social media. Lack of direct face-to-face communication leads to talking from a soapbox, negativity, narcissism, and the out of hand discussion on topics that should not be brought up at the dinner table.

You give a lot of yourself. How do you stay grounded and "keep your bucket full"?

It took a long time for me to learn and it's been my biggest challenge. I have learned to give from my saucer not my cup. This means that I give the overflow and always make sure my cup is full. If find myself giving from my cup, then I make sure to step back. I keep my cup full because I can only serve others fully when I have completely served myself.

What are the characteristics of a philanthropist?

A philanthropist wants to have a lasting impact on society; they want to see a lasting change in the world.

What is the legacy that you'd like to be remembered for?
Giving without expecting to receive. This means that I want
to support members of the community and share success with
those members. Supporting the community means helping to
develop individual members through mentoring, volunteering, and spreading kindness to others.

**The number of people that you're influencing on a daily
basis is impressive. What advice would you give to women
looking to do what you do?**
Trust your gut and always get caught telling the truth. That
way, you can always give generously and sincerely without
expecting to receive. When you are following your passions
and living right with yourself, people will seek you out.

What personal mantra keeps you inspired?
"Every day, think as you wake up, 'Today I am fortunate to be
alive. I have a precious human life. I am not going to waste it.
I am going to use all my energies to develop myself, to expand
my heart out to others; to achieve enlightenment for the
benefit of all beings. I am going to have kind thoughts
towards others, I am not going to get angry or think badly
about others. I am going to benefit others as much as I can.'"
- Dalai Lama XIV

Introspection

How much of your time do you spend socializing during the day? (This includes social media.) 10% 30% 50% 70% 100%

Do you think increasing the amount of time that you truly spend connecting with people would enhance your life? Why or why not?

List one group or community that you are currently a part of and the reasons why you enjoy it:

community + {social connectedness}

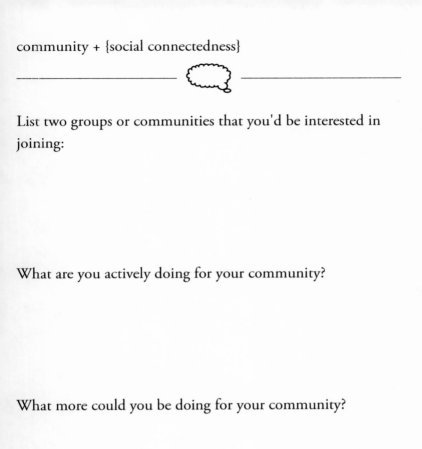

List two groups or communities that you'd be interested in joining:

What are you actively doing for your community?

What more could you be doing for your community?

What organization or causes do you donate your time or money to? Or which ones would you like to?

Suggested Resources

Books:

The Blue Zones: Lessons for Living Longer From the People Who've Lived the Longest by Dan Buettner

Life as a Daymaker by David Wagner

Websites:
- thebluezones.com
- greatergood.berkeley.edu

Apps:
- Meetup
- Planet Goodwill: 365 Simple Ways to Spread the Love

Mary Pokluda's info:
- Website: bumblebeepa.com
- Facebook: facebook.com/bubblebeepa
- Twitter: @bumblebeePA

*"Be your own kind
of beautiful."*

- Unknown

Beauty + {Nutrition}

*This final chapter is meant to be a tool for a professional consultation and/or lesson. To get the most out of the information, I recommend that you consult with a professional to create a customized self-care regimen.

Skin

Our skin is our largest organ. It is vulnerable to earthly elements and our lifestyle choices, so it is important to nurture and protect our skin. Failure to do so can result in having undesirable skin conditions, including skin cancer –the fifth most common cancer. By simply protecting yourself and avoiding over-exposure to the sun, it's also one of the most avoidable cancers.

With thousands of skin care products on the market promising to make us look younger and healthier, it can become overwhelming to know which to choose.

The first step in your skin care journey is to visit an esthetician. An esthetician performs specialized procedures with skin care products and tools and can analyze the current state of your skin.

Maggie Miley Kelly has been a licensed esthetician and educator for 18 years. She's a skin care guru and takes on a holistic approach to beauty. She makes skin care understandable and do-able.

Q + A
with Maggie Miley Kelly

When factoring in age, what should we look for in a serum?

A good serum for your 20s will be hydrating, antioxidant, and oil-free for oily skin.

For women in their 30s, I always recommend to look for plant stem cells and peptides, which are great for preventing and correcting the signs of aging. This is also a good age to introduce a good eye cream into your regimen for that very delicate skin around the eyes. (It's thinner than a piece of paper!)

In your 40s you may begin to notice a bit of a loss of elasticity, and lines and spots may start to appear, so a good treatment serum should include firming agents and skin lighteners.

Once you hit your 50s, it's a good time to begin using increased levels of Vitamin C and retinol to keep the skin's cellular turnover moving and to stimulate collagen production.

Women in their 60s and older should consider a nutrient-rich, thicker moisturizer for the ultimate protection against water loss.

What key ingredients should we look for with the following skin types and concerns?

Dry/dehydrated Skin: Hyaluronic acid, which is a moisture-binder, which holds 1000 times its own weight in water! Also look for plant stem cells, antioxidants and SPF protection.

Oily skin: Use salicylic acid in a small amount—1 to 2% can help balance oil production and prevent breakouts. Titanium dioxide is a sheer sunscreen protection, which can feel better on oily skin.

Combo skin: Look for salicylic acid and hydrators like hylauronic acid.

Sensitive skin: You'll want products with anti-inflammatories, like bearberry extract and kojic acid.

Fine lines: Lactic acid, plant stem cells and peptides can plump the skin by stimulating collagen production.

Deep lines: Retinol (which exfoliates and stimulates), vitamin C, plant stem cells, peptides, and all-important ingredients for deep lines.

Dark under-eye circles: Vitamin K!

Under-eye puffiness: Look for firming and smoothing ingredients such as plant stem cells and peptides.

Age spots: Lightening agents such as kojic acid, bearberry extract and vitamin C are what you'll want to look for.

Acne: Salicylic acid, benzoyl peroxide and oil-free moisturizers will help acne-prone skin.

Large pores: For large pores, look for Retinoids and AHAs (alpha hydroxy acids) such as lactic acid.

Uneven skin tone: Antioxidants, Vitamin C

Saggy skin: Firming agents such as peptides and plant stem cells will help fight sagginess.

Blackheads: Blackheads need to be extracted out of the skin. Have a deep-pore cleansing facial with a licensed esthetician.

For home care, oil-free formulas are best for those prone to blackheads.

Dullness: Brighteners and lighteners such as Vitamin C, Arbutin, and Kojic acid will help fight against dullness.

Redness: For redness, look for anti-inflammatory agents and brightening agents such as Vitamin C, green tea, and licorice extract.

How do you deal with a blemish that seems to have taken residence on your face?

Use a spot treatment with salicylic acid and benzoyl peroxide. Apply before bed every night. If it persists for longer than a week, see a licensed esthetician for a gentle extraction or zapping with a high-frequency wand.

If you must attempt an extraction on your own at home, do so after a bath or shower when skin is softened and clean. Wrap clean fingertips with cotton or gauze and apply gentle, gradual pressure to the area around the blemish. Don't force it - this can make it worse and risks scarring! When you've extracted all that is ready to come out of the blemish, apply a spot treatment with antibacterial salicylic acid.

What other daily habits do you feel contribute to healthy skin?

Drink lots of water with lemon, limit intake of soda and sugary treats, cleanse skin every single night, get a good night's sleep whenever possible, exercise to get circulation flowing and spend time in nature!

There are so many types of exfoliators out there, it's overwhelming. Please help clarify.

There are physical and chemical exfoliants. Physical exfoliating products contain microbeads or grain-like ingredients to slough off dead skin cells. Chemical exfoliants use enzymes, AHAs or BHAs (alpha hydroxy acids or beta hydroxy acids), that dissolve the dead skin cells. Chemical exfoliants can be combined with other ingredients to also speed up cellular turnover (the rate at which new cells replace the old).

What must we know about sunscreen?

Always look for physical blocks, which are titanium dioxide and zinc. These ingredients block the UV rays from penetrating your skin and reaching the deeper layers. Research has found these ingredients to be much safer for your skin and system than chemical sunscreen ingredients, such as avobenzone, octocrylene, octinoxate, and homosalate. Look for SPF 30–this is the gold standard for protection. If you plan to spend a day outdoors, apply a full shot glass of SPF 30 to your entire body and face, and reapply every few hours.

Is it okay to mix skin care brands? Why or why not?

Most skincare companies will say that their products are formulated to work synergistically, meaning there is a greater benefit if you use them together. I believe that if you find your favorites from a few different lines, it's okay to mix them. The only products that work are the ones that you'll actually use! It's more about the ingredients than the brand, so you will want to make sure you have a balanced regimen.

Why are treatments with skin care professionals important?

Professional treatments can assist in achieving results that you may not be able to get at home. I am an absolute believer in deep-pore cleansing each month or so, customized peels that can target your specific concerns and conditions, and professional brow shaping. Also, a licensed esthetician (skincare professional) can educate on ingredients and products for home use so it's not so confusing with a thousand choices.

What's your favorite quote?

"The first wealth is health." - Ralph Waldo Emerson

Skin Analysis

— it's always changing

Determine your skin type:

☐ Normal–balanced hydration, clear complexion, smooth ✗
☐ Oily–shiny, enlarged pores, blemishes
☑ Combination–areas of dry and oily skin typically in T-zone
☐ Dry–flaky, lackluster, invisible pores
☐ Sensitive–redness, itching, hot, hyper-reactive

Determine skin your texture:

☑ Smooth
☐ Scarred
☐ Bumpy
☑ Fine lines/wrinkles

Now let's address your specific concerns: (rank biggest to smallest concern)

__1__ Oily
_____ Dry
_____ Sensitive (redness)
__4__ Aging
_____ Acne
__2__ Unwanted skin tones (hyper-pigmentation)
_____ Rosacea
__3__ Under-eye dark circles
_____ Under-eye puffiness
_____ Loss of elasticity (sagging)

After identifying your type, texture, and concerns, you can
shop for ingredients that will bring balance back to your skin.

SKIN CARE SHOPPING LIST:

oil-free day lotion — hyaluronic acid
'skin binding ingr.

gentle exfoliating cleanser

Serum = evening out skin tone
and/or aging

Skin Care Steps

You'll want to choose your products based on your skin type, texture, and concern.

1. Cleanse
Cleansing is the most fundamental step of proper skin care. Every day we are exposed to pollution and adverse elements that can cause a number of skin issues.

2. Tone
Toning can refresh, hydrate, tighten pores, balance pH, and prep the skin for serums and moisturizers. The two main toners are 1. hydrating 2. astringent.

3. Exfoliate
Exfoliating removes dead skin cells. This helps with cell renewal—bringing new skin forward. The two main types of exfoliators are 1. manual 2. chemical.

√gentle

4. Treat
Treating the skin is addressing a specific skin concern by using a concentrated serum or mask. √

5. Moisturize

Moisturizing helps hold water in the outermost layer of the skin. Moisturizers also aid in protecting our skin from environmental aggressors, which can cause skin issues and aging. The two main types of moisturizers are 1. water-based 2. oil-based.

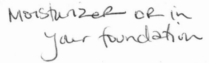

↑ AM   PM

6. Protect

Using a sunscreen is the single greatest skin care step we can do to protect our skin from damage, aging, and disease.

Moisturizer or in
your foundation

beauty + {nutrition}

Notes

Notes

Face Chart

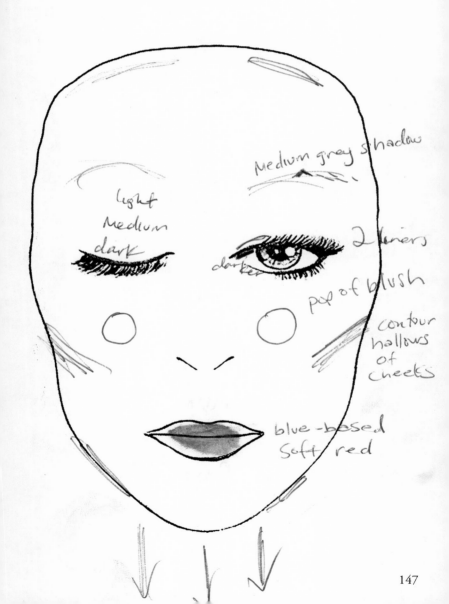

Medium grey shadow

light
Medium
dark

darker

2 liners

pop of blush

contour
hallows
of
cheeks

blue-based
soft red

Makeup

Here's the deal: makeup is subjective. While I might think someone's makeup is pretty, you may not. Everyone has a different makeup style, and everyone should. That's what makes us individuals.

So go ahead, use any color and technique you want to. It's *your* face.

But you would benefit from knowing the following:
1. Skin type and texture
2. Skin's undertone and unwanted tones
3. Facial shape, including face shape, eye shape, bone structure, brow shape, and lip shape

Let's begin to create your customized makeup routine!

My skin type today is: Combo

My skin texture today is: Fine lines

What is your skin's undertone? You're either a warm (yellow), cool (pink), or neutral (beige).* _warm_

*Lift something orange to one side of your face and something blue on the other side. What color makes the skin look more awake and lifted and which color makes the skin look more drained and dragged? The color that makes your skin look awake and lifted is typically the undertone of your skin. If you can't decide, you're likely a neutral undertone.

Let's look at what unwanted skin tones you want to correct. An example would be correcting skin hyper-pigmentation like sunspots.

Areas I want to correct: _freckles_

Let's study eye shape. There are two different eye shapes:

Mono-lid   and   Bi-lid

My eye shape is: _Mono-Lid_

Let's look at what features you want to enhance. Examples could be lip shape or cheekbones.

Features I want to enhance: _eyes, brows, and cheekbones_

Once you get to know your canvas, you can apply makeup in 15 steps:

1. Primer	6. Brow definer	11. Highlighter
2. Eyeshadow	7. Corrector	12. Blush
3. Eyeliner	8. Foundation/Base	13. Bronzer
4. Lash Curler	9. Concealer	14. Lip Color
5. Mascara	10. Contour Color	15. Finishing Products

MAKEUP SHOPPING LIST:

translucent loose powder
to reduce shimmer

Shadow colors:
black
Pewter
ashy brown
purple
beige/taupe for crease

Matte light beige/bone
for brow bane

Eyelash curler —
pocket curler
Sephora

Tinted Moisturizer
Sephora Laura Mercier (oil-free)
Aveda
Sephora Stila-Sheer color tinted

151

Notes

blush —
  plum tone (cool)
  also look for Matte
    formulations

under eye corrector —
  Benefit erase paste
  #2

Brows —
  Medium grey Shadow

Bronzer —
  Laguna by NARS

Notes

Foods for Beauty

There's the saying, "we are what we eat." Well it sucks, because it's true. What we put inside our bodies will most definitely show up on the outside.

Being mindful of our diet and knowing what foods have beauty benefits are key to aging gracefully.

Blueberries, spinach, tomatoes and walnuts are just a few examples of the foods that we can eat that will improve our skin's health, giving us a healthy glow and radiance.

In David Wolfe's book, *Eat for Beauty*, he details how to nourish the body from the inside out. He explains that yoga, sleep and the psychology of beauty all play a part in whole body care.

Like the premise of this workbook, you will not achieve true beauty (and experience your true self!) until you are in balance with your mind, body, and spirit.

beauty + {nutrition}

FOODS FOR BEAUTY SHOPPING LIST:

Suggested Resources

Books:

Organic Body Care Recipes: 175 Homemade Herbal Formulas for Glowing Skin & a Vibrant Self by Stephanie L. Tourles

Bobbi Brown Makeup Manual: For Everyone from Beginner to Pro by Bobbi Brown

Websites:
- davidwolfe.com
- mybeautyphd.com

Apps:
- Beautylish
- Fooducate–Healthy Weightless, Food Scanner and Diet Tracker

Maggie Miley Kelly's info:
- Website: complexionsoncarter.com
- Facebook: facebook.com/ComplexionsOnCarterSkincareBoutique
- Twitter: @mileymaggie

" ...the truth will set your free."

- John 8:32

Evaluation + {Self} Actualization

Hello, gorgeous. Congratulations on completing this workbook!

Let's take a short survey to assess how balanced you currently are.

– I am satisfied with who I am.	Yes	No
– I am happy with the life that I am leading.	Yes	No
– I truly love myself.	Yes	No
– I am grateful nearly every day.	Yes	No

I am doing my best to take care of my:

– Physical health	Yes	No
– Emotional wellness	Yes	No
– Intellectual (brain) health	Yes	No
– Spiritual connection (with yourself and/or your Higher Power)	Yes	No

I am mindful of my relationship with:

– Money	Yes	No
– The people in my life	Yes	No

— I have created my own definition of success.	Yes	No
— I am passionate about something (anything!) in my life.	Yes	No
— I take time to travel and explore (locally and/or out of state).	Yes	No
— I am socially connected and am part of a community.	Yes	No
— I believe that I am a beautiful person inside and out.	Yes	No
— I like Julie Swenson.	Yes	No

If you've answered "yes" to 10 or more of these questions, then you are on your way to achieving a beautifully balanced life. If you have answered fewer than 10, go back to the chapters in relation to the "no", and give some additional thought to how you could improve that area of your life.

{Self} Actualization

In closing, I want to commend you for writing your truth. I chose to use the white Chrysanthemum flower throughout this book because it symbolizes truth and honesty. When we "speak" our truth, we are one step closer to self-actualization: fully knowing and accepting who we are, and living on purpose.

Suggested Resources

Books:
The Four Agreements: A Practical Guide to Personal Freedom by Don Miguel Ruiz

The Last Lecture by Randy Pausch and Jeffrey Zaslow

Quiet: The Power of Introverts in a World That Can't Stop Talking by Susan Cain

Boundaries: When to Say Yes, How to Say No to Take Control of Your Life by Henry Cloud, John Townsend

Outliers: The Story of Success by Malcolm Gladwell

The Paleo Manifesto: Ancient Wisdom for Lifelong Health by John Durant

Mindsight: The New Science of Personal Transformation by Daniel J. Siegel

Man's Search For Meaning by Victor. E. Frankl

Julie Swenson's info:
- Websites: julieswensonbeauty.com, mybeautyphd.com, makeupannex.com
- Facebook: facebook.com/beautyinbalancebook
- Twitter: @julieswensonphd
- Instagram: @julieswensonphd
- Pinterest: pinterest.com/julieswensonphd

Thoughts